SURVIVAL
AND
TRIUMPH

THE MARONITE CHRISTIANS OF LEBANON

A. J. Abraham

Survival and Triumph
The Maronite Christians of Lebanon

by Dr. A.J. Abraham

Library of Congress
LOC #2015948334
ISBN 978-1-55605-462-4

EBook Version 978-1-55605-463-1

Wyndham Hall Press
5050 Kerr Rd.
Lima, OH 45806

Coat of Arms of the Maronite Patriarchate

Also by A. J. Abraham

Lebanon at Mid-Century, Maronite-Druze Relations in Lebanon 1840-1860: A Prelude to Arab Nationalism

The Cross and the Crescent: An Ecumenical Perspective

Islamic Fundamentalism and The Doctrine of Jihad

The Lebanon War

Lebanon: A State of Siege (1975-1984)

Lebanon in Modern Times

The Eternal War: A Psychological Perspective on the Arab-Israeli Conflict

Another Look: One God and Three Faiths

CONTENTS

PREFACE

This book is based upon a paper I wrote some time ago entitled: "Maronite Culture, Lebanon, and the Arab World," in *Transnational Perspectives,* vol. 15, no. 1, 1989, pp. 1-4, and reprinted in *The Challenge*, June 10, 1990.

This study is also based upon two dire needs at present. The first is to present a brief and easily readable, clear and concise history of the Maronite church, its people, their beliefs, as well as their impact upon Lebanon, their homeland and nation, the Arab World, and well beyond into the Third World.

Secondly, there are several books on the Maronite Church, its history and culture, but most of them are too convoluted, speculative, overly complicated, confusing or complex for the average lay person to read. I hope to simplify that problem in this text.

Also, all too often in some of those studies the Maronites have been put on the defensive, and maligned by some writers who have interpreted the historical sources out of context without authentic evidence or based upon conjecture to produce anti-Maronite perspectives on some key religious and political issues.

I have presented in this study the Maronite perspective and opinion on what they believe to be true about their faith and nation and, therefore, I have given them the benefit of the doubt where evidence to the contrary is lacking.

For far too long the Maronite church and nation have been forced to survive in a hostile environment; both Christian and Moslem. To their great benefit and exceptional or extraordinary achievement, the Maronites have clearly defended themselves against all threats and accusations, by providing an ideology and generating principles to confront victimization, neglect, and prejudice.

Those basic principles may be summarized as follows:

1. The Maronites generated an open minded attitude of live and let live long before freedom of religion became an accepted ideology in the West.
2. Their interpretation of scripture was aimed at understanding and co-operation.
3. The Maronites developed a liberal attitude towards other faiths free of any hostility.
4. Their church gave assistance to all in need regardless of faith or ethnic origin—the highest level of Christian humanism.
5. They sought autonomy, freedom and independence for all Lebanon.
6. And, they have accepted modern culture and values within Christian-Catholic moral limits, beliefs and values.

I hope this small volume will clarify the intricacies inherent in the history of the Maronite people and their nation for current and future generations. My hope is that this study will also help the Maronites to find great pride and prestige in their faith, to propagate the importance of Saint Maron and his church, and to endear themselves to that heritage as the Irish people have done for their patron Saint Patrick.

ACKNOWLEDGEMENT

I wish to express my gratitude to Mr. John A. Cardello, scholar and educator, writer and media critic, broadcaster and columnist who has continually supported my academic endeavors and edited my works; and to my wife Esther R. Abraham whose continuous assistance and support in my research and writing has been a spectacular achievement.

In Memory Of

AL-AMIR YUSUF RUKHUS MATTAR

My grandfather whose transition from a traditional culture to a modern society was accomplished with great dignity and honor.

History is replete with the names of men who founded religions, who created nations, and established states: however, only a few men initiated all three—Saint Maron of Lebanon stands out among them in epic proportion.

INTRODUCTION

The Near and Middle East is the land of prophets and kings. The kings are almost all gone and their empires and kingdoms dissolved or have been thrown upon the trash-heap of history. The prophets are all dead and they are still where they fell; but, the religions they initiated remain with us to this day.

The three western religions, Judaism, Christianity and Islam are all desert religions that began in the Near East and grew to maturity there but they have also influenced the entire world. They are all monotheistic beliefs meaning they believe in only One True God for all mankind who revealed Himself to them, teaching them His rules of conduct for a proper and moral way of life.

For this study, we are concerned only with Christianity which centers on the life, career and death of Jesus of Nazareth.

Jesus of Nazareth, the Messiah, the Christ (Christos) was born in full light of history when Rome was master of the known world. The city of His birth was Bethlehem, in the Roman province of Palestine. He lived there for most of His life; He preached, taught, and worked miracles by the power contained within His divine spirit, and, consequently, He gained a large and faithful following. His short career, about three years, ended tragically,

He was arrested and tried by a Jewish court for

blasphemy; He was turned over to Pontius Pilot, the Procurator (governor) of Judea, for a second trial as a seditionist and possible revolutionary. He was condemned to death by the Roman authorities during the reign of Tiberius Caesar. And, thus, He was crucified among criminals on a hill named Golgotha (Skull Place), outside the city of Jerusalem.

After His death, His apostles and disciples claimed that they saw Him on numerous occasions, as many as five hundred at one time. For forty days, they sat, talked and ate with Him and they physically touched Him. Death claimed no victory over Him! His apostles and disciples believed that He was the expected Messiah and the one and only Son of the Living God.

The Life of Jesus was recorded in the Gospels (the Good News) to preserve an account of His life and teachings for future generations. The Gospels or New Testament are attributed to Mathew, Mark, Luke and John, and were never intended to be duplicates or copies of one another because they were addressed to different intellectual and cultural audiences—the Hebrew, the Near Eastern, the Greek and the Roman. They were written between 64 and 105 A.D. so that they encompass the Apostolic Age (the first two-thirds of the first century) and the Sub-Apostolic Age (the last one-third of the first century) and, later, they were interpreted by the Church Fathers well into the second century and beyond.

The Gospels have had a wide-base of appeal to all—a universalist creed, bridging the gap between the Hebrew faith, Greek logic (philosophy) and Roman Law (legalism) to create a new moral way of life and to supersede all other religions.

As Christianity spread throughout the world, the Syrian region became largely Christian by the fourth century and an Ecclesiastical Age (about the 4th to the 6th century) was inaugurated. The work of the Church Fathers who augmented, explained and expounded, propagated and promoted the Christian faith proved to be extremely successful for a very long time.

The church was the most important and powerful institution of that age. Christianity had institutionalized itself—from a small secret gathering place at first for security to a highly organized church (ekklesia/Ekklesia Katholike)—and it continued to grow in proportion and strength into a highly influential church and community. And, a patriarchate was established as a center of authority, the seat of a bishop, and regional authorities. There are five patriarchates that date back to the early church—Jerusalem, Antioch, Rome, Alexandria, and Constantinople of the Byzantine Empire which held authority deep into Syria and North Africa. Some churches in Syria were in agreement with Constantinople, while others followed their own national/regional leadership in the Near East. The strongest of these independent churches would eventually become the Maronite Church of Lebanon. Later it would join with Rome as an equal but independent entity with its own patriarch.

The Ecclesiastical Age was also an age of patriarchal

rivalries, religious heresies, and Christological controversies all of which split the eastern churches into numerous divisions over the human and divine nature of The Christ.

Docetism (Dokesis) meaning “semblance or appearance” argued that Jesus, the biological Christ, was a form of “phantomism” or an “optical illusion” and, therefore, they denied His humanity. For them, Jesus was only pure divine spirit. His human nature was declined to an almost unimportant position.

From that point of view, it was a simple jump to the monophysite doctrine meaning only one nature of the Christ. The opposite point of view is known as diphysite (dual nature) the complete human and divine natures in one person. The monophysite heresy was condemned for depicting and declining the human life and suffering of Jesus as “fictitious,” or fraudulent. It was, finally, rejected by the Council of Chalcedon (451 A.D.).

In a final attempt to reconcile the two interpretations on the nature of Jesus, a new theory, a compromise, accepting the separate natures but only one divine will (thelima) was propagated as monothelism. This doctrine was rejected by the Lateran Council of 649 A.D. and the sixth ecumenical Council of Constantinople (680-681 A.D.). Today those views no longer agitate the intellectual heritage of the Catholic, Orthodox or Protestant churches—they are all diphysite.

Long before the Council of Chalcedon and the Lateran Council came to their conclusions on the nature of Christ, the

Maronite Church led the way to those perspectives although they were often accused of the opposite. Therefore, one may conclude that the Maronites were Chalcedonians even before the council of Chalcedon convened.

CHAPTER 1
THE EASTERN CHURCHES

Most Christians in the United States and Europe are familiar with the Roman (Latin) Catholic, the Protestant, and the Eastern (Greek) Orthodox Churches. Very few people in the west are aware or have any knowledge of the Christian Churches of the Near and Middle East. One reason for this is that for centuries the Christian West lost sight of the eastern churches that came under Moslem rule. Only brief contacts during the time of the Crusades had an ephemeral and sometimes negative effect on both. Those eastern churches survived under Islamic rule and became part of the Arab World, but they retained their faith. Unfortunately, often they were in conflict with one another over doctrinal issues, that fact, indeed, facilitated the Moslem conquest of the Near East for Islam because the Arabian religion was much easier to comprehend too many, and free of religious controversy at first— that is prior to the rise of Shi'ite Islam and, later, other Moslem minority sects.

The Eastern Catholic Churches are sometimes designated as the "Oriental Churches" to distinguish them from the Orthodox Churches of the East (the Greek, Russian, Slovak, Syrian and others). All the Eastern Catholic Churches recognize the primacy of the pope, the Vatican, and the Latin

Catholic Church. They all maintain the same morals and obedience to the Holy See in Rome; and all their sacraments are totally valid as is their Holy Mass (the main ceremony).

The Eastern Churches consist of five rites that began in the Apostolic Age, even before the establishment of the Western (Latin/Roman) Rite.

The word "rite" means "ceremony" or observance and signifies different liturgies and languages; each rite has its own *Canon Law*. But, some other churches remained independent of both Orthodoxity or Catholicism as "independent or regional" churches, or as churches of "national or ethnic origins." Their religious traditions are recognized and accepted by both the Orthodox and Roman Catholic Churches as totally valid rites.

The Eastern Catholic or "Uniate" churches include the Byzantine, Alexandrian, Chaldean, Armenian and Antiochene rites. For this study, we are only concerned with the Antiochene rite.

Each of the churches of the east is under the authority of its patriarch who is the "chief pastor" of his church. He can hold authoritative church councils (synods) of the bishops to determine the proper doctrines and practices of his church.

Antioch, the city that gave the name Christian to the followers of Jesus of Nazareth, was a main center of eastern Christianity and hosted as many as three patriarchs at one time for different rites. The city is associated with Saint Paul's mission and may be called the first "capital" of early

Christianity prior to Constantinople and Rome. Unlike ancient Greek and Roman humanism which was rooted in nationality and ethnicity, Antioch radiated a universal Christian concept of humanity to all peoples.

By the late second century A.D., the Syrian (Suriani), Syriac speaking church, split into two divisions—the East Syrian and the West Syrian groups. The West Syrian Church was monophysite and the East Syrian Church was diphysite. The Maronite Church was always diphysite, stressing the dual nature of The Christ. The Maronite Church would eventually be centered in Lebanon, and its patriarch accorded the title of Patriarch of Antioch and All The East, thereby filling the vacancy at Antioch and reconstructing or completing the current five Holy Sees.

CHAPTER 2

SAINT MARON AND THE ORIGINS OF HIS CHURCH

For about sixteen hundred years a strange group of Christians called the Maronites have lived in geographic Syria and Lebanon. Not much has been known about their early history, nevertheless, a lot has been written about them; truly, they have intrigued historians, scholars and church leaders throughout their long and enduring existence. Consequently, many theories have been advanced about their origins and beliefs, some intellectually and politically hostile to them. No doubt, however, they are part of the Eastern Catholic Churches; and they are composed of the indigenous peoples of the Lebanon. Their church was founded by the legendary Saint Maron.

Saint Maron (Maroun/Maro in Syriac means "the small, lord," ca. 350-410 A.D.) was an ascetic and enigmatic monk-priest. According to Professor Philip K. Hitti, in his comprehensive work, entitled *Lebanon In History,* the facts of his life can be put or "condensed into one brief paragraph." But Maron's influence was monumental!

The fundamental reference or "earliest sources" on Saint Maron are the works of Theodoret (ca.393-485), bishop of

Cyrrhus (Cyr/Qurush/Qurus), in his monumental study entitled: *Historia Religiosa* (Religious History of Syriac Asceticism); and in the undated letter or epistle of Saint John Chrysostom (d. 458 A.D.) who wrote to Saint Maron soliciting his blessing and prayers while inquiring about his well being. He addressed the letter to "Maron, priest and ancharite (hermit)."

Of the Moslem Arab historians and writers Saint Maron and the Maronites are briefly mentioned but yield no additional information of value.

Saint Maron first lived in a district of Syria called Syria Second (Syria Secunda) or Afamiyah (Apamea /Apameus) of the Romans and Byzantines. It is now called Qal'at al-Madiq, erected as a Christian capital about 452 A.D., on the Orentes River, and it is located between Antioch and Qurus (Qurush/Cyrrus) where Maron died about 410 A.D. It is there where Saint Maron planted the seeds of Christianity by converting a pagan temple into a church and its adherents to Christianity, thereby establishing "the first Maronite church," called Maron's House (Bet Maroon/ Ar. Bayt Maroun).

Saint Maron has been credited with miracles, cures and exorcisms, during his career. Also, he helped the mentally troubled or those with psychological ailments by merciful actions, patience and humane care—so it is said he treated "body and soul." He was a great teacher as well, quite charismatic in that he stressed concepts of justice, charity (generosity), self-control (morality) and called for Christian humanism for all, even if many were not Christians or were Christian schismatics or pagans. Thus, Christian humanism found root in Syria replacing the older forms of Greek and Roman humanism.

Third and fourth century Syria was a crossroads of the world for trade and intellectual controversy. Peoples from as far south as Arabia and as far east as Persia filtered into the region; certainly, Arabian tribes found new homes in Syria and Lebanon, such as the Qaysi and Yamani confederations. They brought with them several heterodox Christians creeds which were planted in Greater Syria. Syria was also a land of hermits and monks. The Maronites were only one group among many but, eventually, they won over many of the other Christians to the Chalcedonian and Catholic creed, by peaceful means. But it was not easy!

While the Maronites fiercely clung to their diphysite beliefs about the dual nature of the Christ, the monophysites had many adherents from Egypt into Syria and as far north as Armenia. Some scholars maintain that Theodore of Pharon, an Arabian Christian, might have introduced the monophysite doctrine to the Maronites, but that remains wild speculation.

Secondly, Byzantine Emperor Heraclius (r. 610-641 A.D.), it is said, devised an expedient to resolve the monophysite-diphysite controversy. Thus, he introduced a new doctrine which was called monothelism. In essence it maintains the two nature theory but insisted on only one will (thelema) between God the Father and Jesus Christ. In 628

A.D., the Emperor visited the Maronite monastery in Syria and some scholars believe that he introduced Monothelism to its monks. This is also just weak conjecture.

We have no direct evidence from the Maronites that the monophysite or monothelite doctrines were accepted by them, in fact, the opposite is true because they were attacked for their beliefs. What seems probable, and quite possible, was that many heterodox groups lived among the Maronites in safety and freedom under a "live and let live policy" of the church.

There were also many monasteries and monks in Syria at that time; and the name Maron was not uncommon. Some non-Maronite monks may have taken that name as a "praise name" or to identify with Maron's monastery and community. No doubt, there may have been great confusion between Saint Maron and other schismatics, ascetics, heretics or anchorites who called themselves Maron. Those non-Maronites may have been monophysites and monothelites.

In the Ecclesiastical Age (ca. the 4th-6th centuries A.D.) an issue was raised in church controversies over the unity that exists between God the Father and Jesus Christ; this was based on the Gospels indicating that Jesus prayed to His Father before raising Lazarus from three or four days of death; and, then again, at the Garden of Gethsemane where Jesus asks His Father about His immanent execution. The church agreed with Jesus Himself implying that "thy will be done." The two independent beings, Father and Son, were in perfect harmony of wills—there could never be any discord, dissonance, divergence, incompatibility, or inconsistency between God The Father and Jesus Christ.

This was the Maronite perspective and it was probably misunderstood as some kind of monothelism by others who may have confused themselves in their writings.

What lends further credence to the Maronite claim to Catholic Chalcedonian belief was that they were attacked by the monophysite Jacobites and other schismatics or heretics.

After Saint Maron's death, his disciples carried his body to a place near Apamea (Afamiyah) on the Orentes River (nahr al-Asi) and built a monastery to commemorate his life and work. Their disagreements with the Jacobites led to a massacre of about 350 Maronite monks on or about the monastery in 517 A.D., and its subsequent destruction. (Emperor Justinian, The Great (527-565 A.D.) restored the walls of the original monastery, but by then the Maronite migrations into Lebanon had begun.) A renewed conflict in the second half of the next century made northern Lebanon the "permanent home" of the Maronites.

The Jacobites continued to flourish in Syria for several centuries. They take their name from Jacob Bardaus (Ya'qub al-Barda'i (the saddle maker) who became an ordained bishop in Edessa (ca. 541 A.D.) and died about 578 A.D. There is no doubt that the Jacobites were monophysite and opposed Maronite beliefs; but, they gained no victory over the Maronites.

A greater or stronger threat to the Maronites came from Emperor Haraclius (r. 610-641 A.D.). After routing a Persian foray into Syria in 628 A.D., Heraclius visited the Maronite monastery to discuss his concept of monothelism with the Maronite monks. The Maronites rebuffed both his theory and his veiled threats against them.

There should be little doubt about it. The Maronites were besieged and attacked verbally and physically for their beliefs and their Chalcedonian stand. Their choice was simple: to fight, to escape to a safer location, or to submit. They chose the first two options.

Lebanon (ancient Phoenicia) offered a far better place of refuge because of its high mountains. It had an Arab Christian population which would eventually "amalgamate" with or into the Maronite sect. The roots of the Christian faith in Lebanon can be traced back to the time of Jesus of Nazareth. The Gospels inform us that Jesus traveled to Tyre and Sidon and of His dialogue with a Phoenician woman. (Some Gospel specialists believe that the Mount of Transfiguration may have been the Cedars of Lebanon. And, the Acts of The Apostles tell us that Lebanese ports, such as Sidon, were jumping-off points for the missions of the Apostles. So, Lebanon proved to be ideal at first for the Maronites. But, defense and survival come first.)

In the later sixth and early seventh century, a new powerful group appeared in western Syria called the Maradah by the Byzantine scholars, and the Jarajimah by the Arabs and Syrians. Not much is known about them; their origins are obscure and confusing. From their name two theories of their origin have been assumed. The ancient Semitic stem for their name, m-r-d, means “to rebel” or “to resist” while the Persian word Mard refers to a man who is a valiant warrior. Thus some other scholars believe they were descendents of the ancient Medes of Persia (Iran).

They may have been monophysites or monothelites in faith but this remains uncertain. We know that they were Christians but, certainly, not Maronites. More likely they were Orthodox Christians for the Byzantine rulers called them the “Bronze Shield” of their empire, in regard to their wars with the Arabs.

The obscure and semi-independent Jarajimah’s (Jurajimah/ Jurjumah) place of origin was Amanus (al-Lukkam) and the Taurus range. They were mercenaries or soldiers of fortune, marauders or raiders in Byzantine Syria, and they held-off the Arabian advance for a long time as the Arabs encroached upon the Byzantine Empire’s possessions.

During the eighth century, the Moslem Caliph al-Walid (r. 705-715) launched a major campaign to destroy the Maradites and their capital al-Jarajimah. Thereafter, Syria quickly fell to the Umayyid dynasty and its Caliphate (650-750 A.D.) and then, they began the Islamification of Syria and brought about the almost complete eclipse of Christianity there.

The Mardaites entered Lebanon and by the middle of the eighth century they had become Maronites in faith. And, a new phase in the history of Lebanon would be inaugurated under the Maronite Patriarchate.

CHAPTER 3

THE MARONITE PATRIARCHATE OF ANTIOCH

The history of the Maronites as an independent political force or nation begins with the election of John Maron (Yuhanna Marun/Joannes Maro, d. ca. 707 A.D,) to the vacant see of Antoich. Other patriarchs in the east also claimed that see but they were distant from it, some as far away as Constantinople, and unable to occupy it. Only the Maronite Patriarch claimed and held unbroken authority there, and thus, he was recognized by the other Christian churches and the Moslem states that occupied the Near East. To this day, the Maronite Patriarch holds the title of Patriarch of Antioch And All The East. That has completed the reconstitution and restoration of the original Holy See of Antioch; and, the Maronite Patriarchs were recognized and thus legitimated by Constantinople, the Ottoman Empire, and Rome.

St. Maron was the founder or father and patron of the new sect but it was Yuhanna (John) Marun (Maron) who was the architect of the church, patriarchate and nation. We know much more about him than we do about St. Maron, but in some sources an apparent confusion exists between them because of their names. But, also, we have some Maronite sources on John Maron and his church that shed light on both of them and enables us to make more accurate inferences about them.

Among the earliest Maronite writers on their sect and its origins, heroic battles, and foreign relations with the powers is Jibrail Ibn al-Qila'i (d. 1516). Ibn al-Qila'i's major works are *Madiha 'ala Jabal Lubnan* (Panegyric/Praise on Mount Lebanon) arid Tabkit Kull man Zagh 'an al-Iman (Rebuke/ The Status of Each One Who Deviated From The Faith). Although his historical works betray a few errors, they remain extremely important in reconstructing the history of Lebanon. Patriarch Istifan al-Duwayhi's (L. Aldoensis, 1624-1704) *Ta'rikh al-Maruniyya* (History of The Maronite Community/sect) examines the history of the Maronites. He is still regarded as the father of Maronite historiography. His major work on the evolution of the office of the Maronite Patriarch *Silsilat Batarikat al-Ta'ifa al-Maruniyya* (The Chain of The Patriarchs of The Maronite Sect) takes primary place for showing the continued evolution of that office.

What we can say with heightened accuracy is that Patriarch John Maron was elected with clear national and community related distinctions. He was born in Sarum near Antioch, studied both Syriac and Greek, and joined the Maronite monastery on the Orentes. It is said that he pursued his studies in Constantinople but disagreed with some of the views of its orthodox patriarch on the papacy.

About 670 A.D., John Maron was appointed Bishop of al-Batrun in northern Lebanon. Fifteen years later, in 685

A.D., he rose to the rank of patriarch and built a monastery there. He defended the Maronites of Lebanon from both the orthodox Byzantine forces and the surge of Arab Islam. The patriarch's staunch defense of the Maronites made them a powerful "autonomous nation." When Justinian II's forces proceeded into Syria and destroyed the Maronite monastery in 694 A.D., they then invaded Lebanon but were routed by the Maronite forces at Amyun in the Kura district which remains largely Orthodox Christian to this day. The Arab advance was held in check on the coast and, therefore, the interior mountains remained insulated and isolated from Moslem rule. John Maron, patriarch from 685-707 A.D., also entrenched his people in the Qadisha valley for safety and both his church and nation were fused in their desire for autonomy, religious freedom and, later, independence. From their highland stronghold the Maronite faith and nation spread into the Near East and to the island of Cyprus.

According to the work of a Jacobite Patriarch, Dionysius Tell-Mahri (Denis Tell-Mahre) John Maron was elected to the patriarchate of Antioch in accordance with the "Antiochene Constitutions." This is cited in the *Histoire* de Michel le Syrien, ed. by Chabot and published in Paris in 1903. If this is correct, and there is no evidence to the contrary, then John Maron is the only patriarch who was "democratically" elected to a post vacant for over one hundred years (609-742 A.D.); although other churches may use the same title, only the Maronites were recognized as such.

Furthermore, Patriarch John Maron organized the hierarchy of his church, spread the faith, and incorporated other peoples into his nation-state. This included some people who once called themselves descendents of the Phoenicians and the Mardaites. And, some Arab scholars referred to the inhabitants of Mount Lebanon as "Sha'b Maroun," (The People of Maron/ Maron's People) or the Maronites.

The high mountains of Lebanon could provide security to a certain extent; but, a strong defense is also critical at times. The Byzantine Empire's possessions in the Near East were finally laid to rest by the Arab forces. But, a new challenge to the Maronites would come from Islam and the Arab Empires and, later again, by the Crusaders.

As professor Philip K. Hitti states in his monumental work entitled: *History of Syria. Including Lebanon and Palestine:*

> To the Syrian Christians infant Islam could not have appeared as entirely alien or exotic; in fact it must have appeared more like a Judaeo-Christian sect than a new religion.

However, some of the Christian communities were not in any agreement with that view. They saw Islam as a heresy or as a new religion. Nevertheless, most of the Christians of Syria and Lebanon did not see the Moslem faith as a threat or as an enemy.

At first the Maronites viewed the Moslem advance as a political quest for domination over the region, a form of political rivalry with the Byzantine Empire for resources and trade, not a conflict between religious ideologies. But, in fact, the main theme of Islam is the unity of God (Allah) and this would eventually discount the divinity of Jesus, his death by crucifixion, and his self-resurrection. (For more on Christian-Moslem relations see; *Another Look: One God and Three Faith* by A. J. Abraham.)

Thus, for the most part, the Maronites fared well under Umayyid rule (650-750 A.D.), for no major or permanent hold or encroachments occurred; but under the Abbasid rule (750-1258 A.D.) the Moslems became more militant after a tax revolt at al-Munaytirah near Afqah took place (759-760 A.D.) well within the Lebanon range.

There were many motivational forces in operation to launch the Crusades; some factors include personal salvation, acquisition of new lands, control over religious sites, and control over the trade routes to the Near East. However, religion was the cementing force for the conflict on both sides. Some recent scholars believe that the Crusades were a response by the Christian West to the Arab invasion of Western Europe. The primary sources of both western and Arab scholars on this are mostly in agreement. Both Steven Runciman's classic study, *A History Of The Crusades,* in three volumes, and Amin Maalouf's *The Crusades Through Arab Eyes,* clearly show the political and religious overtones in the confrontation. But for the Maronites, they found themselves caught in the middle of the conflict.

While the Crusaders controlled much of the Lebanese

coast, the interior of Lebanon was still autonomous until the thirteenth century when the Mamluks gained the advantage on the coast, and the Crusaders fled into Maronite territories for refuge. Some Maronite princes (amirs) and notables (ayan) had been allies of the Crusaders and were regarded and treated as lords by them.

But many of the other Maronites in the mountains had tried to maintain good relations with the Moslems by remaining neutral. This all ended in 1267 when northern Lebanon was pummeled by the Moslem forces. Between 1289 and 1291 the entire Lebanese coast was conquered by the forces of Islam. Therefore, many of the remaining Crusaders and their Lebanese allies fled into the high mountains of Lebanon, and joined the Maronite church; other fled to Cyprus and Rhodes and still others went to parts of southern Europe. (Some Lebanese families still trace their origins to the European Crusaders such as the Salibis and Frangiehs, and many others.)

CHAPTER 4
THE MARONITE-LEBANESE INTERREGNUM

The departure of the Crusaders from the Near East did not leave Lebanon or the Maronites isolated or alone. Commercial contacts and trade continued to grow, the rivalry between the European Powers for influence and trade among Lebanese religious sects or groups progressed, and the Maronites and Rome began to initiate contacts for religious unity.

The long march of Islam finally broke-up along the northern reaches of the Middle East and numerous Christian communities became the subjects of different Arab States. Some were engulfed by Islam and Arabism; but Lebanon had a window to the West, its coastline. Nevertheless, the Christians of the Near and Middle East became "islands" in a vast Moslem "sea."

There was brisk trade along the Lebanese coast. The Europeans took much from the Arab East in food products, and manufactured goods as they did in Crusader times. Trade with France and the Italian city-states flourished.

The Middle East had a lot to give to the West but not only in products. Arab scholarship proved to be one major source of Europe's Renaissance. There had never been a Dark Ages in the East so that Hellenistic science and culture filtered into Europe along with trade. The Maronites were, of course, involved in all those activities and transactions.

Of the European states interested in Lebanon and the Maronites the French took the lead, followed by the English and Italians. The French stressed the religious link of Catholicism with the Maronites more so than the other states.

But, contacts between Rome's Vatican and the Maronites had been long and enduring. From the beginning of their contacts, the Maronites held pride of place among the other Christians of the East in that they were the first Christians there that Rome looked at and sought union with for reasons of faith and trade with the Italian city-states. (This also made the Maronites quite wealthy.)

The first reported contact between the Maronites and Rome occured about 1134 A.D. when Maronite Patriarch Gregory of Halat (1130-1141) initiated negotiations with a papal legate about the possiblity of union with the Roman Church.

The main issue in subsequent negotiations and meetings was the foolish revival of accusation against the Maronites for being Monothelists which was condemned by the sixth Ecumenical Council in 681 A.D. It died hard, for it took a long time until Pope Leo X, in 1510, recognized the "orthodoxity" of the Maronites, something the Maronites had always claimed. Finally, a papal bull fully recognizing the Maronite rite was issued and sent to the patriarch, ending the controversy.

By 1625, the Maronite Church had expanded to include several eparchies and dioceses throughout the mountains and into the cities. And the military power of the former Mardaites was coupled to the ecclesiastical authority of the bishops and the patriarch for security and protection. That was something that Europe could understand as the "Maronite nation," and deal with politically in future relations.

The main issue in the future negotiations between Rome and the Maronites involved the process of unity - how to combine the Roman rite with the Antiochian rite while maintaining the future independence of both. This has been referred to as the Latinification or Latinization of Eastern Christianity. Much of that was completed by church synods or councils. There were many meetings but, finally they achieved recognition in rites with great dignity and style while preserving the autonomy of the Antiochian Maronite rite.

The first synod aimed at unity began in 1580 and again in 1596 and progressed to new ones in 1598; in 1608, Father Giralimo Dandini went to Mount Lebanon and helped organize a synod at Qannubin to "upgrade" the Maronite establishment along modern or western lines. The culmination of all this activity was the Synod of Luwayza in 1736. The meeting gave the Maronite Church and its patriarch the force of pontifical authority in its laws and in its own decrees. This was quickly approved by Pope Benedict XIV in 1741. And, the patriarch was given the authority to translate the catechism of the Roman Rite (a comprehensive summary of church doctrine) into Syriac and Arabic, consequently completing the union. A permanent mission of the Maronite Church was sent to Rome and soon after its arrival it established a college there. It taught Syriac and Arabic and completed a common Bible translation. That was a major achievement of Pope Gregory XIII, in 1885.

French contacts with Lebanon and the Maronites go far back in time. They were both religious and strategic in part, and they involved European rivalries and commercial expansion. They also involved many other Lebanese communities, Christian and Moslem.

A tradition relates that as far back as the reign of Louis IX (1226-1270), the Maronites who had supported the Crusader Kingdom of Jerusalem were accorded "protection" by the French. This commitment was confirmed by Louis XIV (1643-1715) and his royal successors to protect Catholicism in the Near East and to promote trade and commerce. The Capitulations (Lat. for chapters: capitula/ Ar. imtiyazat ajnabiyah) regulated economic relations between the East and the West and they helped revive Europe's economy after centuries of stagnation.

But, of even greater importance for Lebanon, the political relationship between France and Lebanon grew stronger with the appointment of the Khazin family as French vice-counsels in Beirut. France had become both friend and protector of the Maronites.

Some of the foregoing material is well known from European sources, but the domestic and foreign relations of Lebanon from the fall of the Crusader kingdoms to the rise of the Ottoman

Empire to its heights in the nineteenth century are far more complicated. Our basic source for that period are William R. Polk's *The Opening of South Lebanon, 1788-1840*; Iliya F. Harik's, *Politics and Change in a Traditional Society, 1711-1845;* and more recently Richard van Leeuwen's, *Notables & Clergy in Mount Lebanon, The Khazin Sheikhs & the Maronite Church. (1736-1840).*

Several important developments in domestic policy occurred in that space-time continuum. First of all, the Maronite church and establishment became a dynamic force with energetic leadership, organizational strength, and mass support capable of leading a major insurrection for the independence of Mount Lebanon in the nineteenth century. Also, the feudal structure of Lebanon (the iqta' system) was modeled on French feudalism; Lebanon's notables (the 'ayan) and the amirs became lords of the land, but their tenants were never serfs. This situation produced an expansion of Maronite tenant farmers into Druze territory and would prove to be problematic in the future. Two other important developments occurred as well.

One can be called Maronite ecumenism, in that the Maronite Church welcomed European religious communities such as the Franciscans and other members of religious organizations including the Orthodox Christians (al-Rum) who use Greek in their Liturgy, and members of other Eastern Churches. Later, protestant sects and groups were also welcomed. The church and Maronite community also protected persecuted minorities such as the Syrian Druze, Moslem Shi'ites and the Armenian Christians.

Secondly, the growing power of the Maronite clergy in

secular affairs led to conflicts with the Ottoman Empire, its appointees (the pashas/administrators), the local notables, and secularists and that would project Lebanese autonomy into the first Arab nationalist revolt for the independence of Mount Lebanon from the still overpowering Ottoman Turkish Empire.

CHAPTER 5

THE MARONITES, LEBANON AND THE OTTOMAN TURKISH EMPIRE

The Ottoman Turkish Empire stood like a mighty colossus with one foot in Europe and the other foot in the Arab World. It brought parts of south-eastern Europe and the Arab States into its own world. Of the two, it has been said, that "the Arab World was far more important to the Turks." The Ottoman Turks would rule the Arab lands for over four hundred years (1514-1918 A.D.); it proved to be one of the largest and most enduring empires in western civilization.

The year was 1514 when the mighty army of Sultan Salim I (r. 1512-1520), "the grim," unleashed his powerful forces against the Persian Empire and the Mamluks of Egypt. In 1516, Salim won a stunning victory against his enemies, first on the plain of Chalderon and then again at Marj Dabiq north of Aleppo. Soon after, the smaller Arab States collapsed like a house of cards, capitulating quite quickly. And, thus they remained in the Port's embrace for centuries.

The Turkish Sultan (Authority) inherited an area with many different ethnic and religious groups. Consequently, the Turks proved to be flexible and great administrators, perhaps similar to the Romans, ruling both directly and indirectly over many faiths. But, Lebanon with its numerous sects would prove to be a formidable problem and, eventually a thorn in the Empire's side. Lebanon was a microcosm of the entire Near and Middle East under semi-autonomous or completely autonomous religious sects. The Turks did the best they could to rule over a diverse population but they were no fools. By the beginning of the nineteenth century, Lebanon was already in political ferment, tumult, and "turmoil."

The Ottoman conquest of Syria and Lebanon was hailed as a deliverance from the corrupt rule of the Mamluks; and Sultan Salim quickly received a delegation of Lebanese princes (amirs) who pledged their allegiance to him in return for continued autonomy. That was the best conditions the sultan could get, for Lebanon's communities were "Independent Minded," that is, each sect had its own leaders and the sultan knew that very well.

The Sunnite Moslems more strongly supported the sultan because they both belonged to the same Sunni sect of Islam and, they saw the Turkish Empire as a successor state to the great Arab Caliphates. The Shi'ite Moslems and the Druze were more cautious since they were seen as heritics by the Sunnite establishment. The Maronite Christians retained their hold on the mountains, and the Orthodox Christians held firm on the coast. Every group was recognized within their own religious domain. (The Turkish system was known as the millet system (Ar. millah/ religion/ nationality) or confessional identity).

This imposed peace of subjugation did not last long; the

harmony established at first was broken by the Druze in 1544 in a conflict with the Ottomans. The Druze rose up against the sultan's regime under Prince Fakhr al-Din al-Mani II (1590-1635) whose combined Druze army had Maronites and other Christians in it; He revolted against the Turks with promised European support that never materialized. Fakhr al-Din II is, nevertheless, still considered to be the founder of modern Lebanese nationalism.

Lebanon remained quiescent for a while under Shihabi rule. Amir Bashir al-Shihab II (1788-1840), a Maronite, held the reins of power tightly, although he had considerable opposition both domestic and foreign. His major achievement was that he was recognized as the most prominent amir in Mount Lebanon, the ruler (al-Hakim) by domestic princes and the foreign powers, including the Ottoman Empire.

When his rule ended Lebanon slipped into chaos and civil war. The period between 1841 and 1860 was one of the darkest in Lebanese history. It threatened the possible extinction of the Maronites at the hands of the Druze and the Ottoman Empire.

There are numerous studies of that period placing the blame for the Maronite-Druze civil wars on different groups. No doubt, there were many factors that motivated the conflict in the mid-nineteenth century. The classic study of the Ottoman Empire's involvement in Lebanon is Caesar E. Farah's *The Politics of Interventionalism in Ottoman Lebanon, 1830-1861;* for a complete political history of modern Lebanon in the nineteenth and twentieth century's see: A. J. Abraham's *Lebanon In Modern Times*; and the uniqueness of Ottoman Lebanon is depicted in Kamal Salibi's *A House Of Many Mansions.* In addition, original sources for the period include: Colonel Charles Henry (Spencer) Churchill's *The Druze and the Maronites Under Turkish Rule: From 1840-1860; and Mount Lebanon: A Ten Years Residence 1842-1853,* in 3 volumes, and James L. Farley's *Massacres in Syria.*

Several Arabic reference touch upon the occurrences as well, they include: Antun Dahir al-Aqiqi, trans, by M.H.Kerr, *Lebanon in the Last Years of Feudalism, 1840-1860;* Tannus al-Shidyaq, *Kitab Akhbar al-Ayan fi Ta'rikh Jabal Lubnan* (A Book on The Notables of Mount Lebanon); Mansur Tannus al-Hattuni, *Nubdhah Ta'rikhiyah fi al-Muqata' at al-Kisrawaniyah* (A Historical Note on The Kirawani Districts); Philippe al-Khazin's *Lamahat Ta'rikhiyah* (Historical Glances); Yusuf As'ad Dagir, *Batarikiyah al-Maruniyah* (The Maronite Patiarch); and, Hussayn Ghadban and 'Arif Shaqra, *Al-Harakat fi Lubnan ila 'ahd al-Mutasarrifiyah* (The Events in Lebanon up to the Time of the Mutaarrifiyah). There are additional references to the conflict in Lebanon in the British and French archives in their ministries of foreign affairs.

There are many complex themes in the history of the Lebanese conflict. Some scholars see the conflict as a result of foreign intrigues and involvement by Britain and France in the affairs of the Ottoman Empire citing British support for the Druze and French support for the Maronites. Others see it as a clash between the Maronite and Druze sects as a consequence of the Maronite farmers in the mixed districts challenging Druze feudal lords to end feudalism, and still others maintain that the crisis resulted from local instances such as trespassing or accidental events causing tempers to flair.

From a religious perspective the Druze believed that Bashir al-Shibab III (1840-1842) distributed territory belonging to them to his relatives, and Patriach Yusuf Habash (1823-1845) supported the hakim's right to do so. The Druze became convinced that there was a plot hatching against them and backed by the Maronites. In the mixed Maronite-Druze villages, the Druze lords believed that the Maronite peasants were rejecting Druze feudal authority which could result in the end of their feudal power.

While there is some truth in the foregoing explanation of the Maronite-Druze civil wars of 1841, 1845, and 1860, most writers believed that it was an outbreak of religious intolerance or sectarian rivalry. This was, however, not the case or the cause.

During the first outbreak in September of 1841, the alignment of forces on both sides had Christians and Moslems; in the second clash in April of 1845, the conflict took on the appearance of a sectarian struggle with the Orthodox Christians and the Greek Catholics joining the Maronites. In the first civil war they were on the Druze side fearing Maronite domination. Also, the Shi'ite Moslems joined the Druze fearing the militantly Sunnite Moslem Turks would take revenge upon them for supporting the Maronites in the first war. Most of the Sunni Lebanese were "neutral" supporting the "law and order" of the Turkish regime.

When the Druze were promised immunity from persecution as heretics by the Sultan's regime, a third civil war in May of 1860 took place in which the Maronite forces were defeated and about 12,000 Maronites were "put to the sword." (For a more detailed study of that conflict see: A. J. Abraham's *Lebanon at Mid-Century, Maronite-Druze Relations in Lebanon 1840-1860: A Prelude to Arab Nationalism.*)

The Ottoman regime was under extreme pressure when modern nationalism began to impact upon its ethnic and religious minorities, in the early nineteenth century. In the Balkans, the Serbs revolted for greater autonomy in 1804; then, the Greeks rose up in revolt in 1821 and with European help won their independence. In a similar way, the Maronites under the authority of their Patriarch Yusuf Habash (1823-1845) and his bishops raised the standard of revolt in the mixed districts in 1841 and then in the Lebanese mountains for the independence of the Lebanese province. But, the Maronite establishment's quest to create an independent Christian Arab amirate proved to be a monumental disaster. The slogan, "the Patriarch is our Sultan" proved to be too weak for national unity. The Turks continued to tighten their hold on Lebanon; they believed the loss of Greece and the

Balkans, on the periphery of the Ottoman Empire was tolerable; the loss of Lebanon or any part of it, in the heart of the empire, was too dangerous for their future. So, they agreed with the European Powers: Great Britain, France, Russia, Austria and, later, Italy to create a new autonomous regime for Mount Lebanon (Jabal Lubnan).

From the patriarch's point of view, this new regime was just another temporary arrangement short of full independence, but it succeeded in providing Lebanon with about sixty years of peace and prosperity.

After long, protracted, discussions between the European Powers and the Ottoman Empire, a new statute for Mount Lebanon was approved by all. The region would be ruled by a governor-general called the mutasarrif who could never be a Maronite or Druze; the Porte (the Sultan's government) recognized the independent mindedness of both groups. The document provided peace and stability until the beginning of the First World War and was known as the Reglement Organique which broke-up Lebanon into seven semi autonomous districts (qada), under the mutasarrif.

The mutasarrif was recruited from the Ottoman citizens of the Catholic faith whose loyalty would be to the sultan. He instituted a Central Administrative Council (CAC/AC)/majlis idarah) to represent all the sects in a 7:5 ratio of Christians to Moslems. It proved to be the first representative government in the Arab World, and it was freely elected, and could advise the governor-general.

The governor-generals had their job cut out for them

since they ran into conflicts with the patriarchs from 1854 until 1915 over the temporal authority they had, and also with Lebanon's national hero, Yusuf Bek Karam (d. 1889) as well as others.

When World War One began, the Ottoman Empire was on the side of the Central Powers (Germany, Austria-Hungary, and Italy) and against its former allies. Now, the struggle for Lebanese freedom began to take a definite shape. A new world order was in the making in the Near East, and the Maronites would take and hold a prominent place in Lebanon's struggle for independence.

CHAPTER 6

THE MARONITES, FRENCH RULE AND THE MODERNIZATION OF LEBANON

The outbreak of World War One ended all arrangements that had governed Mount Lebanon and the Lebanese province. And, furthermore, in the Arab lands of the Turkish Empire, the first stirrings of a still disjoined Arab Nationalism began to form. In Lebanon, however, the Maronite Church led the way towards the acquisition of complete independence, and Arab-Lebanese nationalism (Lebanonism).

The Ottoman administration was no doubt well aware of those tendencies and sent Jamal Pasha with a contingent of troops to Lebanon to quell any opposition to Turkish rule. That may clearly explain his "iron fisted" policy towards even the least or slightest sympathy towards the Arab cause or the French forces.

In Jamal's first meeting with Maronite Patriarch Elias Hawayyik (Hoayek/1898-1931) and his bishops, Moslem and Christian notables and members of the Central Administrative Council (the CAC/AC), Jamal tried to invoke or enlist their support; but, he was quickly dismayed and rebuffed. Thus, the CAC was dismissed and a new one appointed. The patriarchate was put under extreme scrutiny and constant observation. Nevertheless, in time, it was the CAC and the patriarchate that would bring Lebanon to complete independence from the still powerful Ottoman Empire.

The best detailed study of the CAC and its role in the quest for Lebanese independence is an article by James L. Simon entitled: "The Role of the Administrative Council of Mount Lebanon in the Creation of Greater Lebanon, 1918-1920," in the *Journal of Third World Studies*, vol. XIII, no. 2, Fall, 1996, pp. 119-171; and the classic study by Stephen H. Longrigg, *Syria and Lebanon under French Mandate*, as well as George Haddad's *Fifty Years of Modern Syria and Lebanon*. On the Arab perspective there is Antun Yamin's *Lubnan fi al-Harb* (Lebanon During the War); K. T. Khairallah's, *Le Problem du Levant, Les Regions Arabes Liberees* and Chekri Ganem's *Comite Libanais De Paris, Memoire Sur La Question Du Liban.*

During the First World War, in a series of secret agreements, England and France decided to divide the Arab lands of the Ottoman Empire among themselves. The emerging states became class A Mandates of the League of Nations. They were to be guided to political independence, but no time-table was ever set. For the Maronites this was just another temporary arrangement short of full independence.

The Moslem and Christian members of the CAC, realizing the lack of clarity regarding the end time of the

Mandate, began to oppose this new form of "international" colonization. Several missions were sent to Paris to plead the Maronite case for the immediate independence of Lebanon; and, several committees were set up in the Near East, Europe, the United States and South America, to propel that quest. Secret societies in Lebanon grew including The Covenant (al-Ahd) and The Cedars (al-Arz). Overseas, committees were set up in San Paulo, Brazil (1913) and in Buenos Aires, Argentina (1916). In Egypt, Yusuf Sawda published a study on Lebanon called *Lubnan fi al-Ta'rikh* (Lebanon in History), and Antun Gemayal organized the Alliance Lebanese D'Egypt in Cairo; In Brooklyn, New York, al-Amir Yusuf Rukhus Mattar of Kiserwan, encouraged the Maronite community to evoke Lebanese independence through church meetings and social and political organizations (clubs).

The road to independence proved to be a rocky one at best. Within Lebanon there was a division in thought between those who wanted the expansion of Mount Lebanon to include the non-Christian areas to create Greater Lebanon; but, most Sunnite Moslems wanted all Lebanon to be attached to Syria and called for a Greater Syria. The problem was resolved in Paris when the borders of modern Lebanon were established or set in accordance with the ancient maps of Phoenicia, consequently recognizing the Phoenician origins of the Lebanese people.

The Mandate over Lebanon was comprehensive and designed to modernize Lebanon, but independence was not included in any of its articles. Although its reforms were beneficial to all, French overtones were very clear. France was more concerned with Great Britain's influence and role in the Near East and not with the wishes of the Maronites or any of the other pro-independence minded Lebanese citizens.

At first several administrators were sent to govern Lebanon under the Permanent Mandate Commission until High Commissioners could be appointed. These High Commissioners had French interests at heart, and failed to understand that Lebanon was not a backward area in a colonial empire to be ruled "in military style." The French attitude aggravated both Christians and Moslems alike.

During the period of French rule, a modern constitution was drawn up. It was the initiative of Michel Chiha, a Greek Orthodox by birth, who insisted that all sects be included and treated with dignity and equality. The details were outlined in Paris and promulgated in Beirut. A new parliament came into existence; it was supported by the former CAC members. Lebanese leaders accepted the constitution and self rule but also called for the end of the Mandate, or at least to set a date for its termination. The French would not acquiesce.

Opposition to the Mandate grew in strength and coalesced about the office of Patriarch Antun (Antoine/Anthony) Peter 'Aridha (1932-1955) and the Maronite clergy. 'Aridha reached out to all Lebanese, Christian and Moslem alike calling the Mandate an "outdated temporary arrangement" that was no longer useful to any Lebanese.

While all could agree on the need for total independence, there was little agreement on the vacuum of power that would follow a French departure. Numerous articles in the Lebanese press and some journals debated the issue of representation; finally, a Lebanese Formula was agreed upon by all parties and sects. The President would be a Maronite; the Prime Minister would be drawn from the Sunnite Moslem community; the Speaker of the House (the Parliament) would be chosen from the Shi'ite sect, and the Minister of Defense would be a Druze. This was based on a census taken in 1932. And, all diplomatic positions and government posts would be assigned to various sects so that no group would be kept out. (A Christian or Moslem presidency is not called for in the Lebanese constitution. But, in order to avoid a conflict over which Islamic legal system would be the official one in Lebanon, and could dominate the state a Christian presidency would allow for secular law in all general matters, while leaving religious law to each sect in personal affairs. State Law would be in the hands of the lawyers and the parliament, not the religious establishments. Also, a Christian presidency would send a message to the surrounding Arab-Moslem states that Lebanon has an Arab face with dual Christian and Moslem values and culture.)

Added to the Lebanese Formula was the National Pact, agreed upon in the last days of the Mandate; it called for political neutrality in Arab and European affairs. While Lebanon is part of the Arab World, it should not be engulfed in it nor should it be overwhelmed by the West. In fact, nonalignment was the key to a balance of power for future independence in the state. (It should be noted here that the Confessional System of religious representation, the Lebanese Formula and the National Pact were Lebanon's system of checks and balances.)

The Mandate system lasted for the inter war years, and then ended quickly when both England and the United States recognized the independence of Lebanon. During French rule Lebanon made amazing strides into modern times. In general, it can be said that the Maronites were more pro-French than the Orthodox and other Christians or the Sunnites, Shi'ites or Druze. Most scholars believe that that was true because the Maronites and the French were Catholics. But much more can be said about the French-Maronite connection. First of all, Lebanese unity was supported by the French; Lebanon is not an "artificial" state, as some have said, but rather it is a state with a diverse religious and ethnic base, perhaps more like the United States. However, national loyalty is still a problem for the non-Maronites. No doubt, all the Maronites and many from the other sects support a Lebanese interests first policy often referred to at times as Lebanonism.

Also, the Maronites clearly saw the road to modernization in the adoption of French ideas and values. This does not mean, however, that they abandoned Arab or Moslem values or any of their own. No doubt, modernization came to the Middle East from the West. French educational and other institutions always included all the sects. As far as the Maronites were concerned, the limit to copying western culture was an adherence to Catholic culture first in moral and ethical issues.

CHAPTER 7
THE MARONITES AND INDEPENDENT LEBANON

The Maronite Christians as well as many of the other sects in Lebanon found the road to independence uncertain and unchartered, at first. The old realities had to be respected, and the hew ones adhered to at least politically. The Confessional System, the Lebanese Formula and the National Pact protected all the groups equally and preserved the state's freedoms and independence.

Lebanon exists in a precarious balance of power between the religious sects in a Confessional Democracy giving prominent political positions to groups to avoid confrontations between them, while the National Pact existed to control foreign influences and interference in international affairs. The Maronite position has always been to support Arab Nationalism while allowing the independent states to thrive. Lebanon is part of the Arab World, but should not be engulfed in all its problems. A balance of power was the best it could achieve. But, Lebanon is still far from a western or perfect-styled democracy, yet, it did succeed in protecting all its citizens from any single group gaining power over the others, or victimizing or marginalizing any sect. It had, however, built in problems in that it was not a truly secular democracy, something the entire Arab World sorely needs.

On the origins of the Lebanese system of government see the classic study by M.C. Hudson, *The Precarious Republic, Political Modernization in Lebanon;* and Leonard Binder's *Politics in Lebanon*. More recent studies include Hilal Khashan's *Inside The Confessional Mind*; Enver M. Khoury's *The Crisis in The Lebanese System, Confessionalism and Chaos;* Kemal Junblat's, *I Speak for Lebanon;* and Ephraim A. Frankel's, "The Maronite Patriarch: A Historical View of a Religious Za'im in The 1958 Lebanese Crisis," in *The Muslim World,* vol. LXVI, no.3, July 1976, pp. 213-225.

Lebanese political stability results from the structure of the state. The distribution of political posts by religion worked well until it was challenged by some right-wing and left-wing secularists who had been "iced-out" of the political system. Secondly, the National Pact was derived from two negatives. The Moslems would not draw too close to the Moslem World, and the Christians would avoid alignment with the Christian West. Thus, there was no positive foreign policy, or ideological approach for the new nation.

The Confessional System, the Lebanese Formula and the National Pact can be compared to three scales perched on top of one another; on each scale, one tray represents Moslem aspirations while the other scale represents Christian ambitions. As long as the balance remained all went well, and Lebanon prospered. However, the slightest hint of change could bring all three scales crashing down.

In addition to the weakness in the state system, Lebanon has some conditions evident in many other "small states" in the non-western world. These include: factionalism, regionalism, tribalism, sectarianism, parochialism and city-mountain ties that impact the political scene. This makes national unity highly complex making it very difficult for a Lebanese person to be "just Lebanese." It opens the door to wild accusations between the sects and their leaders, and between the regional powers and the central government of Lebanon. With a weak presidency and government, suspicions run high, and the head of state has to prance around numerous groups and individuals to avoid conflicts. This, all together, makes Lebanon susceptible to foreign ideologies and political schemes.

Nevertheless, the Lebanese leaders followed the lead of the Maronite Patriarch in supporting a policy of consensus and cooperation in all important matters. That policy worked well until the late 1950's when the scales of "justice" tipped over because of foreign plots and ploys. Actually, the balance of power and the National Pact were threatened.

Even before independence, Lebanon found itself in a very precarious position because of its location, just north of Mandated Palestine. In Palestine, Zionist Jewish Nationalism clashed with Christian-Moslem Palestinian Arab Nationalism over the region once the British Mandate would be terminated in May of 1948. Fear that a more powerful Zionist entity would take over south Lebanon as far north as the Litani River brought the Patriarchal Office into the

Palestinian crisis, as a defender of Lebanese sovereignty.

Patriarch Antun Pierre ‘Arida of Tripoli seeing that the parties were hopelessly deadlocked, and that a civil war was in the making, tried his hand at conflict resolution. His actions brought upon him and the Maronite community accusations that they were sympathetic to the Zionist cause, or to Zionism. Thus, the Lebanese peace initiatives were challenged from within and from afar by all those who do not want a unique Maronite Christian Arab entity in the Arab World. (These charges of disloyalty to Arab Nationalism were brought about by several anti-Maronite, and anti-Christian politicians in Lebanon to discredit the state and cast the Christians as enemies in the Arab World.)

In his book, *Lubnan al-Ta'ifi* (Sectarian Lebanon), Anis Sayigh, a Lebanese “scholar” quotes a ‘‘questionable source that claims that Patriarch ‘Arida called for the establishment of a Zionist State in Palestine”. Others said that the Maronite-Zionist negotiations produced a treaty recognizing the above mentioned claim. That accusation finally died with the patriarch's death; But throughout his life ‘Arida always “denied the endorsement of such an accord,” or claims.

The details of any negotiations between the patriarch and his designee, Bishop Ignatius Mubarak of Beirut, are quite convoluted at best. Apparently, ‘Arida offered a compromise to both the Zionist and the Palestinians nationalists along the lines of a confessional system and, later, the possibility of a small independent domestic Jewish kingdom within an Arab Palestinian State, sort of like the Vatican in Italy. Both attempts to reach an accord and avoid a civil war were unrealistic and rejected by both parties. The Palestinians and the Zionists wanted all of Palestine for themselves. The unfortunate result of all that for the Maronites is that some Moslems believe that the Maronites were treasonous to Arab Nationalism or perhaps anti-Moslem. That was never the case nor is there any evidence of that!

From the end of the Lebanese Mandate to the mid 1950's, the Lebanese state underwent a major attempt at modernization. New industries were developed, agriculture and trade flourished, and Lebanon became an exporter of numerous goods and products to the region. And, schools at all levels from elementary to universities expanded; The open media kept Lebanon in touch with the region and the world. Almost every ideology found a willing listener in Lebanon. Consequently, Lebanon took giant leaps into the modern world and the future. Lebanon was never a Third World country living off American foreign aid. In fact, poverty and unemployment in Lebanon was lower than in the rest of the Arab World or Eastern Europe and, obviously, the Third World. As measured by the amenities and appliances the poor had at home, and the variety of food they ate, the poor in Lebanon were better off than the middle class in many other Middle Eastern countries. (For more on this see the original article by Joseph Chamie, "Religious Groups in Lebanon: A Descriptive Investigation," in the *International Journal of Middle Eastern Studies*, vol.11, April, 1980, no. 2, pp. 175-187.)

But it is also true that the Maronites and the Sunnites held the lion's share of the wealth in land, industry and businesses.

In Lebanon, there were many millionaires among all sects and they worked well in their economic ventures and partnerships. Yet, the Shi'ite and Druze were less fortunate having been isolated by their own leadership from modern education and values, at times. It is also true that the Maronite and Sunnite birthrates were far lower than the other Moslem sects.

Despite Lebanon's progress, it is not a "fairy-tale land." There were many people among all the sects who were disenchanted with Lebanon's uneven development and progress. And, many of them turned to Arab Nationalism and Arab Socialism as espoused by Egypt's great national leader, Gamal Abd al-Nassar - Nassarism.

President Gamal Abd al-Nassar called for Arab unity across the region and hit a chord among some of Lebanon's Sunnite Moslem community. Lebanon's pro-American president, Camille Chamoun (Kamil Sham'un, 1952-1958) favored alignment with the United States' Eisenhower Doctrine which violated the National Pact and his attempt at re-election brought matters to a head, and led to a civil war. Chamoun's actions alienated the Maronite Patriarch Peter Paul Meouchi (Ma'ushi, 1955-1975) and he made his position known by supporting the Christian and Moslem opposition to the president.

The patriarch called for a new election and for social and

economic reforms and that resonated well with the Christians, Moslems and the Druze. A compromise candidate, who had been neutral during the conflict, General Fuad Chehab (Shihab) became the next president from 1958-1964. He supported new social and economic reforms and his program was known as Shihabism or better yet the Shihabi Method (al-Nahj al-Shihabi). The National Pact was reestablished and neutrality prevailed until 1975.

However, once again, in 1975 the Palestinian problem raised its head in Lebanon and polarized the entire population. The 1948 civil war in Palestine resulted in the forced eviction of about half a million Christian and Moslem Palestinians from their homeland; they ended up in Lebanon in United Nations sponsored refugee camps. (At that time, the patriarch and the Maronite Church called for the immediate repatriation of the displaced people (DP's) to their indigenous homeland.) That situation produced a tremendous burden on Lebanon, the United States and the United Nations and remains that way to this day. Lebanon assisted all refugees, Christian and Moslem alike, and the Maronite Church led the way in helping them. (The majority of refugees were Sunnite Moslems.)

With the rise in the Shi'ite population, in the 1960's, many Lebanese Sunnite Moslems called for the government to grant Lebanese citizenship to all Palestinians to increase Sunnite numbers for Parliamentary representation. Maronite nationalists, including Patriarch Anthony Peter Khoraish (1975-1985), the Druze and the Shi'ite Moslems all rejected this call. They believed it would alter Lebanese demography and was just a Sunnite ploy. And, most importantly, the Palestinians did not ask for Lebanese citizenship for it would destroy their national identity. For the Palestinians foreign citizenship is "Just, a legal fiction."

Nevertheless, most Palestinian refugees remained quiescent until the early 1970's when their camps were taken over by more active Palestinians forced out of Jordan. Lebanon became the only place from which they could conduct their war of liberation against Israel. This brought a devastating Israeli response. (All previous attempts to control the Palestinians commandos on Lebanese soil failed, the border Arab States refused to accommodate the Palestinian resistance, thus, South Lebanon became a major area of confrontation in the never ending Arab-Israeli Conflict.)

On April 13, 1975, the situation exploded when a Maronite right-wing leader, Shaykh Pierre Gemayel (Jumayil), was attacked by what appeared to be Palestinian commandos from the Palestinian Liberation Organization's (PLO's) left-wing Rejection Front. That launched Lebanon on a countdown to destruction and set Lebanon aflame.

A detailed account of the war and its varying issues outlining the battles, conferences and its international affairs can be found in A. J. Abraham's *The Lebanon War*. Most studies on the conflict (1975-1982) blame either external conspiracies or the Lebanese social and political system. Others blame the Palestinian-left united with a Lebanese-left to overthrow the Confessional System, the Lebanese Formula and National Pact which had no place in it for them. And, still others blame the rising Islamic fundamentalist movement called the "Islamic Tendency." There is indeed, some truth in all those perspectives, but to a great extent it was a conflict between a Lebanese right and left. The Lebanese-right wanted a status quo and a Christian Lebanese State in the Free World; the Lebanese-left along with a Palestinian-left wanted a more secular state aligned with the Soviet Union in a way similar to the United States' alignment with Israel. In the long run, Syria took over Lebanon and imposed a piece of subjugation (1985-2011) but Syria stayed too long. The patriarch and his bishops and priest took the lead in unifying all the Lebanese except some Shi'ites in South Lebanon. Patriarch Nasr Allah Pierre Sfeir's initiative succeeded in creating the Cedar Revolution in 2005 and with the help of the United States and France obtained a Syrian departure. (Israel also occupied South Lebanon for too long and, finally, withdrew. This left The Party of God (Hizb Allah) of the Shi'ite sect in charge of the South.)

Post war Lebanon has experienced a major economic recovery, thanks to the leadership of Rafiq Hariri, a Sunnite Moslem Prime Minister, who was assassinated in Beirut (2005). Many Lebanese saw that crime as the work of Syrian intelligence operatives, or the Shi'ites of Hizb Allah whom Syria backed. The United Nations investigation of the crime produced a report that was, at best, inconclusive. (See: *Report of The International Commission Established*

Pursuant to Security Council Resolution 1595 (2005), by Detlev Mehlis, Beirut 19 October 2005).

The report created a major political problem for Lebanon by dividing the country between a Shi'ite Hizb Allah south, and the central government that rallied around the March 14th. Coalition led by the Maronites, Druze and Sunnite Moslems. Hizb Allah attacked the Coalition as a tool of the West that leads only to an ineffectual status quo. By 2007, Hizb Allah was calling itself the champion of Arab and Shi'ite nationalism, against Israel. It was clearly an ally of Syria. When the Maronites called for the rebuilding of South Lebanon, after a brief Israeli-Hizb Allah clash, Shaykh Hasan Nasr Allah of Hizb Allah said that his aim was not to topple the Lebanese government. (But, he sought continued Iranian and Syrian aid.) Thus, the situation remained the same. The March 14th Coalition backed down leaving Hizb Allah the most powerful group to "defend Lebanon" from Israel. (In June of 2008 the United Nations passed GA Resolution 1701 ending the conflict between them for the moment.)

Clashes broke out between the Sunnites and Shi'ites throughout 2008. Hizb Allah obtained additional aid from Syria and Iran and the United States backed the March 14th Coalition in Parliamentary elections. Both American Vice President Joseph R. Biden and Secretary of State Hillary Rodham Clinton visited Lebanon to show support for the Cedar Revolution and Lebanese sovereignty. In August of 2010, the American Congress blocked military aid to

Lebanon for fear that the weapons could end up with Hizb Allah. However, Hizb Allah and Iran called the Beirut government illegal and fanned the sectarian conflict between Lebanese Sunnites and Shi'ites.

In September of 2012, the Pope visited Lebanon as a pilgram of peace and met with all religious leaders. Both Maronite Patriarch Bechara Boutros al-Rahi (2011-present) and Sunnite Grand Mufti Shaykh Muhammad Qabbani joined forces to quell religious and sectarian hostilities. However, religious hostilities increased over an uprising in Syria which turned into a full fledged civil war against President Assad and spilled over into Lebanon.

In September of 2012, Pope Benedict XVI called on the Moslem and Christian youth of Lebanon to work for a better future for all; His call was magnified by the Maronite Patriarch's plea to all for peace and stability. The patriarch sought peace and religious freedom and a return to the neutrality of the National Pact. Nevertheless, Lebanon remains precariously balanced for the foreseeable future.

CHAPTER 8
SOME FINAL THOUGHTS

There is no doubt about it; Lebanon is a unique state among the states of the Middle East. And, the Maronites are a unique people and special group among its citizens. This places upon them, their church, and its patriarch great responsibilities to themselves, Lebanon, and around the world.

Within Lebanon, the Maronites have upheld the high standards of their Catholic-Christian faith. In the face of intolerance and terrorism, they have counseled liberalism and tolerance, and consensus and co-operation.

But, more can be done. The patriarch can meet with other religious leaders, Christian and Moslem, in the Middle East in support of religious freedom, peace, reconciliation, and Arab Nationalism. And, he can reach out to the other Maronite communities in the world as Patriarch Meouchi did when he visited the United States in 1962. He could also meet with the American President and members of Congress in support of Palestinian rights, and to help strengthen American-Lebanese relations.

In many nations around the world, Maronites have greatly contributed to the expansion of human rights, and to fight against poverty and injustice. They have also promoted good will among people in conflict with one another. That is admirable for such a small group.

In regard to the numerous Orthodox churches, it would serve ecumenical purposes for the Maronite Patriarch to meet with their leaders to stress the equal dignity among them and their churches. And, in regard to the great Protestant Churches of the West, it would do well for the Maronite Patriarch to establish a liaison program to stress mutual respect among all Christians. All too often many Protestant denominations still see the Catholic faith from the out-dated, negative, perspective of the Reformation. In Lebanon and in the other Eastern Catholic Churches similar conditions did not exist for a reform movement. The Eastern Churches have remained true to original Christian beliefs and as free as possible from immorality. (Even today, we still do not have any data or statistics on corruption or its extent in the Medieval Latin Church.)

On the international level some scholars maintain that Lebanon is just too small and the Maronites too few and insignificant to be taken seriously. Lebanon has no oil resources like Saudi Arabia, or natural resources to attract the interest and support of the West or the United States. Lebanon's major resources are its people.

For the Lebanese people, and particularly the Maronites, the United States is "more than just an arms merchant to whom they (the Arabs) pay cash." There is a meaningful identity in values between the United States, Europe, and

Lebanon. The Maronite identity has been rooted in the western philosophical values of human dignity, freedom of religion and thought, and a commitment to liberalism and social justice. Consequently, it is in the interest of the United States to remain committed to the survival and sovereignty of Lebanon. By supporting Lebanon and its Maronite people, America is defending its own freedoms and values in an area of the world that is hostile to them. Lebanon should not be put on the back-burners of American foreign policy.

Lebanon is a temple of Janus that bridges the east with the west and brings their peoples together; it remains a beacon of justice and mercy that sheds its light deep into the darkness of the Arab and Third World. Its Maronite population must remain a major exporter of Christian humanism and human dignity into the entire Near and Middle East and well beyond into the Third World.

BIBLIOGRAPHY

In this bibliography some references which are not mentioned in the text are suggested for further reading on the Maronites.

Abraham, A.J., *Lebanon at Mid-Century, Maronite-Druze Relations in Lebanon. 1840-1860: A Prelude to Arab Nationalism,* MD.: University Press of America, 1981.

—.*The Lebanon War*, Conn.: Praeger/ABC CLEO, 1996.

—.*Lebanon In Modern Times,* MD.: University Press of America, 2008.

—.*Another Look: One God and Three Faiths.* MD.: University Press of America, 2014.

Akarli, Engin, *The Long Peace, Ottoman Lebanon 1861-1920.* CA.: University of California Press, 1993.

Atiya, Aziz S., *History of Eastern Christianity,* IN.: University of Notre Dame, 1967.

Attie, Caroline, *The Lebanese Orthodox Community: Historical and Contemporary Perspectives*, MESA, 1990.

Ayer, Joseph Cullen, Jr., *A Source Book For Ancient Church History.* N.Y.: Charles Scribner's Sons, 1952.

Azar, Edward E., (ed.), *Lebanon And The World In The 1980's*, MD., University of Maryland, 1983.

Beggiani, Seely, *Aspects of Maronite History*; VA.: Saint Maron Publications, 2003.

Betts, Robert Brenton, *Christians in The Arab East*, Atlanta: John Knox Press, 1978.

Binder, Leonard, ed., *Politics in Lebanon*, N.Y.: John Wiley and Sons, 1966.

Churchill, Col. Charles Henry (Spencer), *Mount Lebanon, A Ten Years Residence 1842-1852.* 3 vol., London: Sundars and Otley, 1853.

—. *The Druze and the Maronites Under Turkish Rule: From 1840-1860*. London: Bernard Quaritch, 1862.

Dau, Butros, *Religious, Cultural and Political History of The Maronites*, Lebanon: n.p., 1984.

Farah, Cesar E., *The Politics of Interventionalism in Ottoman Lebanon. 1830-1861*, London: I.E. Tauris, 2000.

Farley, James L., *Massacres in Syria*, London: Brosbury and Evans, 1861.

Ganem, Chekri, *Comite Libanais De Paris, Memoire Sur La Question Du Liban,* Paris: C. Pariset, 1912.

Haddad, George, *Fifty Years of Modern Syria and Lebanon.* Beirut: Dar al-Hayat, 1950.

Harik, Iliya, *Politics and Change in a Traditional Society. 1711-1845*. New Jersey: Princeton University Press, 1968.

Harris, William, *Lebanon, A History 600-2011*, Oxford: Oxford University Press, 2012.

—. *The New Face of Lebanon,* Princeton: Markus Wiener Publishers, 2005.

Hitti, P.K., *History of Syria, Lebanon and Palestine.* N.Y.: The Macmillan Co., 1951.

—. *Lebanon In History*, London: Macmillan and Co., 1957.

Hudson, M.C., *The Precarious Republic, Political Modernization in Lebanon,* N.Y.: Random House, 1986.

Huxley, Fredrick Charles, *Wasita In A Lebanese Context, Social Exchange Among Villages and Outsiders.* Anthropological Papers, Museum of Anthropology, University of Michigan #64, Ann Arbor, Michigan, 1978.

Joseph, John, *The Nestorians and their Muslim Neighbors,* N.J.: Princeton University Press, 1961.

Joumblatt, Kamal, *I Speak for Lebanon*, London: Zed Press,

1982.

Jurji, Edward J., *The Middle East, Its Religion and Culture*, Phil.: Westminister Press n.d.

Khairallah, K.T., *Le Probleme du Levant, Les Regions Arabes Liberees*, Paris: E. Leroux, 1919.

Khashan, Hilal, *Inside The Lebanese Confessional Mind,* MD.: University Press of America, 1992.

Khoury, Enver M., *The Crisis in the Lebanese System, Confessionalism and Chaos,* Washington: American Enterprise Institute for Public Policy Research, 1976.

Leeuwen, Richard van, *Notables and Clergy in Mount Lebanon, The Khazin Shiekhs and The Maronite Church, 1736- 1840.* Leiden: E. J. Brill, 1994.

Lewis, Bernard and P.M. Holt, ed., *Historians of The Middle East*, London: Oxford University Press, 1964.

Longrigg, Stephen L., *Syria and Lebanon Under French Mandate*, London: Oxford University Press, 1958.

Maalouf, Amin, *The Crusades Through Arab Eyes,* Paris: Al-Saqi Books, 1983.

Matti, Moosa, *The Maronites,* N.Y.; Syracuse University Press, 1986.

Norton, Richard A., *Amal And The Shi'a, Struggle for the Soul of Lebanon*, Texas: University of Texas Press, 1987.

Phares, Walid, *Lebanese Christian Nationalism*, Colorado: Lynne Rienner Publishers, 1995.

Polk, William R., *The Opening of South Lebanon. 1788-1840.* Mass: Harvard University Press, 1963.

Rahmani, Ignace Ephrem II, Syrian Patriarch of Antioch, *Les Liturgies Orientales Et Occidentales*, in Arabic, Mont Liban: Imprimerie Patriarcale Syrienne de Charfet, 1924.

Ramazani, R.K., *Revolutionary Iran, Challenge and Response In The Middle East, MD., The Johns Hopkins University Press*, 1986.

Runciman, Steven, *A History of The Crusades.* 3 vol., N.Y.: Harper, 1952.

Salem, Elie Adib, *Modernization Without Revolution, Lebanon's Experience,* London: Indiana University Press, 1973.

Salibi, Kamal, *A House of Many Mansions, The History of Lebanon Reconsidered,* Berekley: University of California Press, 1988.

Shehadi, Nadim and Dana Haffar Mills, *Lebanon: a History of Conflict and Consensus,* London: I.B. Tauris, 1988.

Spagnolo, John P., *France and Ottoman Lebanon, 1861-1914.* London: Ithaca Press, 1977.

Tayah, Wadih Peter, *The Maronites, Roots and Identity.* Bet Maroon publishers, Florida, 1987.

The New Testament in Syriac, Great Britain: Oxford University Press, 1955.

Traboulsi, Fawwaz, *A History of Modern Lebanon,* London: Pluto Press, 2007.

Winslow, Charles, *Lebanon, War and Politics in a Fragmented Society,* N.Y.: Routledge, 1996.

Zamir, Meir, *The Formation of Modern Lebanon.* Ithaca: Cornell University Press, 1985.

BIBLIOGRAPHY
(In Arabic)

Abd al-Jabbar, ibn Ahmad al-Hamadhani, *Kitab al-Mughni fi Abwab al-Tawhid wa al-Din* (The Book That Enriches the Entrances to Unity and Faith), Cairo, n.p. 1965.

Abu ‘Aziz al-Din, Najla, *Al-Druz fi al-Tarikh.* (The Druze in History), Beirut: Dar al-Alm I’l Malayn, 1985.

Al-Aqiqi, Antun Dahir, *Lebanon in The Last Years of Feudalism. 1840-1860*, trans, by M.H. Kerr, Beirut: Catholic Press. 1959.

Al-Duwayhi, Istifan, *Ta’rikh al-Ta’ifa al-Maruniyya.* (A History of The Maronite Sect) Beirut: Matba’at al-Kathulikya, 1890.

Al-Hattuni, Mansur Tannus, *Nubdhah Ta’rikhiya fi al-Muqatq’at al-Kisrawaniyah* (A Historical Note on The Kiserawani District), Beirut: n.p., 1884/1956.

Al-Khazin, Philippe, *Lamahat Ta’rikhiyah* (Historical Glances), Cairo: Matba’at al-Fajjalah, 1910.

Al-Masudi, Ali ibn Husayn, *Kitab al-Tanbih wa al-Israf* (A Book of Admonition and Recension), ed. by M.J. De Goeje, Leyden: E. J. Brill, 1898/ Cairo: n.p., 1938.

Al-Shidyaq$_{r}$ Tannus, *Kitab Akhbar al-Ayan fi Ta’rikh Jabal Lubnan* (A Book of Information on The Notables of Mount Lebanon), Beirut: Al-Jami’at al-Lubnaiyah, 1970.

Daghir, Yusuf As’ad, *Batatrikiyah al-Marunniyah* (The Maronite Patriarchate), Beirut: Matba’at al-Kathulikiyah, 1958.

Dahr, Masoud, *Ta’rikh Lubnan al-Ajtima’; 1914-1967* (The Social History of Lebanon, 1914-1967), Beirut: Dar al-Matba’at al-Sharqiyat, 1984.

Daryan, Yusuf, *Nubdhah Ta’rikhiyah fi Asl al-Ta’ifa al-*

*Maruniyah*_ (A Histroical Glance on The Origins of The Maronite Sect), Beirut: Al-Matba'ah al-Ilmiyah, 1919.

Daww, Butros, *Ta'rikh al-Mawarnah al-Dini wa al-Siyasi wa al-Hadari* (History of The Maronites, Religious, Political, and Cultural), Beirut: Dar al-Nahr lil Nashr, 1977.

Fahd, Butros, *Ta'rikh al-Rahbaniyah al-Lubnaniyah bi Fr'aiha al-Halibi wa al-Lubnani* (A History of The Maronite Order in its Branches in Aleppo and Lebanon), Beirut: Matba'at al- Karim, 1963/1981.

Ghadban, Husayn and 'Arif Abu Shaqra, Al-Harakat fi Lubnan ila *ahd al-Mutasarrifiyah* (The Events in Lebanon Up To The Time of the Mutasrrifiyah), Beirut: Matba'at al-Itihad, 1952.

Mas'ad, Bolos, *Al-Majma' al-Baladi* (Le Concile Baladi), Beyrouth: Imprimerie Catholique, 1856.

Mas'ad, Paul (ed.), *Kitab Mukhtasar al-Shari'at* (L'Abrege De La Loi), Beirut: Imprimerie Catholique, 1736.

Yamin, Antun, *Lubnan fi al-Harb* (Lebanon During The War, 1914-1919), Beirut: Matba'at al-Adabbiyah, 1919.

BIBLIOGRAPHY
(Articles)

Chamie, Joseph, "Religious Groups in Lebanon: A Descriptive Investigation," in the *International Journal of Middle Eastern Studies,* vol.11, no.2 April, 1980, pp. 175-187.

Frankel," Ephraim, *A.,* "The Maronite Patriarch: A Historical View of a Religious Za'im in the 1958 Lebanese Crisis," in the *Muslim World.*vol. LXVl. no.3, July, 1976, pp. 213-225.

Shaw, Stanford J., "The Origins of Representative Government in the Ottoman Empire, an Introduction to the Provincial Councils 1839-1876," in the *Near East Round Table.* New York: 1969, pp. 53-142.

Simon, James L., "The Role of the Administrative Council of Mount Lebanon in the Creation of Greater Lebanon," in the *Journal of Third World Studies,* vol. XIII, no.2, Fall, 1996, pp. 119-171.

About The Author

A world class scholar and leading authority on the Near and Middle East and Islamic Civilization, Dr. A. J. Abraham received his B.A. and M.A. from Hunter College and his Ph.D. from New York University. He has lived in Lebanon and has traveled throughout the Near East. He teaches at John Jay College (CUNY) and at New York Institute of Technology.

Professor Abraham's published works have a constant theme, they show us how the world should be, and not to accept it as it is seen. He sees wrong and indicates ways to correct it. His extraordinary vision of humanity rewrites the rules of world order, political conflicts, and religious confrontations to foster peace and justice in a compelling way.

This study and source book chronicles the evolution and history of the Maronite Church and Christians of Lebanon, from their controversial beginnings to the present. The book explicitly and significantly explains the survival of the Maronites caught in the hostile environment of the Middle East. Also it reconstructs the history of Lebanon and its Catholic Church within the context of the Lebanese state and indicates the importance of the Maronites to the region and well beyond.

www.ingramcontent.com/pod-product-compliance
Lightning Source LLC
LaVergne TN
LVHW051017080826
845145LV00009B/2669

* 9 7 8 1 5 5 6 0 5 4 6 2 4 *